UNITED

1999-2000 Yearbook

KU-033-872

PARRAGON

First published in 1999 by Parragon

Parragon
Queen Street House
4 Queen Street
Bath BA1 1HE
UK

ISBN 0-75252-918-8

Fixtures are correct at the time of printing but are subject to change in the event of re-arranged matches.

This independent publication has been prepared without any involvement on the part of Manchester United Football Club or the Premier League.

BANK AND PUBLIC HOLIDAYS 1999-2000

England & Wales
Summer Bank Holiday	Monday, August 30
Christmas Day Holiday	Monday, December 27
Boxing Day Holiday	Tuesday, December 28
New Year's Eve Holiday	Friday, December 31
New Year's Day Holiday	Monday, January 3
Good Friday	Friday, April 21
Easter Monday	Monday, April 24
May Day Holiday	Monday, May 1
Spring Bank Holiday	Monday, May 29

Scotland
Summer Bank Holiday	Monday, August 2
Christmas Day Holiday	Monday, December 27
Boxing Day Holiday	Tuesday, December 28
New Year's Eve Holiday	Friday, December 31
New Year's Day Holiday	Monday, January 3
Bank Holiday	Tuesday, January 4
Good Friday	Friday, April 21
Easter Monday	Monday, April 24
Bank Holiday	Monday, May 1
Bank Holiday	Monday, May 29

Northern Ireland
Summer Bank Holiday	Monday, August 30
Christmas Day Holiday	Monday, December 27
Boxing Day Holiday	Tuesday, December 28
New Year's Eve Holiday	Friday, December 31
New Year's Day Holiday	Monday, January 3
St Patrick's Day	Thursday, March 17
Good Friday	Friday, April 21
Easter Monday	Monday, April 24
May Day Holiday	Monday, May 1
Spring Bank Holiday	Monday, May 29
Battle of the Boyne	Wednesday, July 12

Republic of Ireland
Summer Bank Holiday	Monday, August 2
October Holiday	Monday, October 25
Christmas Day Holiday	Monday, December 27
Boxing Day Holiday	Tuesday, December 28
New Year's Eve Holiday	Friday, December 31
New Year's Day Holiday	Monday, January 3
St Patrick's Day	Thursday, March 17
Good Friday	Friday, April 21
Easter Monday	Monday, April 24
May Day Holiday	Monday, May 1
June Holiday	Monday, June 5

CALENDAR 1999

JANUARY
```
S  M  T  W  T  F  S
            1  2
3  4  5  6  7  8  9
10 11 12 13 14 15 16
17 18 19 20 21 22 23
24/31 25 26 27 28 29 30
```

FEBRUARY
```
S  M  T  W  T  F  S
1  2  3  4  5  6
7  8  9  10 11 12 13
14 15 16 17 18 19 20
21 22 23 24 25 26 27
28
```

MARCH
```
S  M  T  W  T  F  S
1  2  3  4  5  6
7  8  9  10 11 12 13
14 15 16 17 18 19 20
21 22 23 24 25 26 27
28 29 30 31
```

APRIL
```
S  M  T  W  T  F  S
            1  2  3
4  5  6  7  8  9  10
11 12 13 14 15 16 17
18 19 20 21 22 23 24
25 26 27 28 29 30
```

MAY
```
S  M  T  W  T  F  S
                  1
2  3  4  5  6  7  8
9  10 11 12 13 14 15
16 17 18 19 20 21 22
23/30 24/31 25 26 27 28 29
```

JUNE
```
S  M  T  W  T  F  S
      1  2  3  4  5
6  7  8  9  10 11 12
13 14 15 16 17 18 19
20 21 22 23 24 25 26
27 28 29 30
```

JULY
```
S  M  T  W  T  F  S
            1  2  3
4  5  6  7  8  9  10
11 12 13 14 15 16 17
18 19 20 21 22 23 24
25 26 27 28 29 30 31
```

AUGUST
```
S  M  T  W  T  F  S
1  2  3  4  5  6  7
8  9  10 11 12 13 14
15 16 17 18 19 20 21
22 23 24 25 26 27 28
29 30 31
```

SEPTEMBER
```
S  M  T  W  T  F  S
         1  2  3  4
5  6  7  8  9  10 11
12 13 14 15 16 17 18
19 20 21 22 23 24 25
26 27 28 29 30
```

OCTOBER
```
S  M  T  W  T  F  S
                1  2
3  4  5  6  7  8  9
10 11 12 13 14 15 16
17 18 19 20 21 22 23
24/31 25 26 27 28 29 30
```

NOVEMBER
```
S  M  T  W  T  F  S
   1  2  3  4  5  6
7  8  9  10 11 12 13
14 15 16 17 18 19 20
21 22 23 24 25 26 27
28 29 30
```

DECEMBER
```
S  M  T  W  T  F  S
            1  2  3  4
5  6  7  8  9  10 11
12 13 14 15 16 17 18
19 20 21 22 23 24 25
26 27 28 29 30 31
```

CALENDAR 2000

JANUARY
```
S  M  T  W  T  F  S
                  1
2  3  4  5  6  7  8
9  10 11 12 13 14 15
16 17 18 19 20 21 22
23/30 24/31 25 26 27 28 29
```

FEBRUARY
```
S  M  T  W  T  F  S
      1  2  3  4  5
6  7  8  9  10 11 12
13 14 15 16 17 18 19
20 21 22 23 24 25 26
27 28 29
```

MARCH
```
S  M  T  W  T  F  S
         1  2  3  4
5  6  7  8  9  10 11
12 13 14 15 16 17 18
19 20 21 22 23 24 25
26 27 28 29 30 31
```

APRIL
```
S  M  T  W  T  F  S
                  1
2  3  4  5  6  7  8
9  10 11 12 13 14 15
16 17 18 19 20 21 22
23/30 24 25 26 27 28 29
```

MAY
S	M	T	W	T	F	S
	1	2	3	4	5	6
7	8	9	10	11	12	13
14	15	16	17	18	19	20
21	22	23	24	25	26	27
28	29	30	31			

JUNE
S	M	T	W	T	F	S
				1	2	3
4	5	6	7	8	9	10
11	12	13	14	15	16	17
18	19	20	21	22	23	24
25	26	27	28	29	30	

JULY
S	M	T	W	T	F	S
						1
2	3	4	5	6	7	8
9	10	11	12	13	14	15
16	17	18	19	20	21	22
$^{23}/_{30}$ $^{24}/_{31}$	25	26	27	28	29	

AUGUST
S	M	T	W	T	F	S
		1	2	3	4	5
6	7	8	9	10	11	12
13	14	15	16	17	18	19
20	21	22	23	24	25	26
27	28	29	30	31		

SEPTEMBER
S	M	T	W	T	F	S
					1	2
3	4	5	6	7	8	9
10	11	12	13	14	15	16
17	18	19	20	21	22	23
24	25	26	27	28	29	30

OCTOBER
S	M	T	W	T	F	S
1	2	3	4	5	6	7
8	9	10	11	12	13	14
15	16	17	18	19	20	21
22	23	24	25	26	27	28
29	30	31				

NOVEMBER
S	M	T	W	T	F	S
			1	2	3	4
5	6	7	8	9	10	11
12	13	14	15	16	17	18
19	20	21	22	23	24	25
26	27	28	29	30		

DECEMBER
S	M	T	W	T	F	S
					1	2
3	4	5	6	7	8	9
10	11	12	13	14	15	16
17	18	19	20	21	22	23
$^{24}/_{31}$	25	26	27	28	29	30

CALENDAR 2001

JANUARY
S	M	T	W	T	F	S
	1	2	3	4	5	6
7	8	9	10	11	12	13
14	15	16	17	18	19	20
21	22	23	24	25	26	27
28	29	30	31			

FEBRUARY
S	M	T	W	T	F	S
				1	2	3
4	5	6	7	8	9	10
11	12	13	14	15	16	17
18	19	20	21	22	23	24
25	26	27	28			

MARCH
S	M	T	W	T	F	S
				1	2	3
4	5	6	7	8	9	10
11	12	13	14	15	16	17
18	19	20	21	22	23	24
25	26	27	28	29	30	31

APRIL
S	M	T	W	T	F	S
1	2	3	4	5	6	7
8	9	10	11	12	13	14
15	16	17	18	19	20	21
22	23	24	25	26	27	28
29	30					

MAY
S	M	T	W	T	F	S
		1	2	3	4	5
6	7	8	9	10	11	12
13	14	15	16	17	18	19
20	21	22	23	24	25	26
27	28	29	30	31		

JUNE
S	M	T	W	T	F	S
					1	2
3	4	5	6	7	8	9
10	11	12	13	14	15	16
17	18	19	20	21	22	23
24	25	26	27	28	29	30

JULY
S	M	T	W	T	F	S
1	2	3	4	5	6	7
8	9	10	11	12	13	14
15	16	17	18	19	20	21
22	23	24	25	26	27	28
29	30	31				

AUGUST
S	M	T	W	T	F	S
			1	2	3	4
5	6	7	8	9	10	11
12	13	14	15	16	17	18
19	20	21	22	23	24	25
26	27	28	29	30	31	

SEPTEMBER
S	M	T	W	T	F	S
						1
2	3	4	5	6	7	8
9	10	11	12	13	14	15
16	17	18	19	20	21	22
$^{23}/_{30}$	24	25	26	27	28	29

OCTOBER
S	M	T	W	T	F	S
	1	2	3	4	5	6
7	8	9	10	11	12	13
14	15	16	17	18	19	20
21	22	23	24	25	26	27
28	29	30	31			

NOVEMBER
S	M	T	W	T	F	S
				1	2	3
4	5	6	7	8	9	10
11	12	13	14	15	16	17
18	19	20	21	22	23	24
25	26	27	28	29	30	

DECEMBER
S	M	T	W	T	F	S
						1
2	3	4	5	6	7	8
9	10	11	12	13	14	15
16	17	18	19	20	21	22
$^{23}/_{30}$ $^{24}/_{31}$	25	26	27	28	29	

USEFUL ADDRESSES AND TELEPHONE NUMBERS

MANCHESTER UNITED FC

Sir Matt Busby Way
Old Trafford
Manchester M16 0RA

Tel:	(0161) 872 1661
	(0161) 930 1968
Fax:	(0161) 876 5502
Ticket And Match Info:	(0161) 872 0199
Membership Enquiries:	(0161) 872 5208
Club Call:	0891 12 11 61
Official Website:	www.manutd.com

THE PREMIER LEAGUE

16 Lancaster Gate
London W2 3LW

Tel:	(0171) 262 4542

UNITED WE STAND FANZINE

PO Box 45
Manchester M41 1GQ

Alex Ferguson ▶

THE MANCHESTER UNITED STORY

The history of Manchester United Football Club was rewritten last season as Alex Ferguson's team swept all before it en route to an historic Treble of Premiership, FA Cup and European Cup. A knighthood was the wily Scot's reward, while his team – led by swashbuckling Roy Keane and featuring the country's most exciting player, David Beckham – carved a unique place in the sport's record books.

Never before had this clean sweep of domestic and European honours been achieved. And the latter victory was the sweetest of all, coming as it did on the birthday of Sir Matt Busby, the late, great boss who'd first taken United to that peak in 1968. All the managers that followed were measured against the exploits of that

MANCHESTER UNITED FACTFILE

Year formed:	1878
Ground:	Old Trafford, Manchester M16 0RA
Nickname:	The Red Devils
Club colours:	Red, white and black
Manager:	Sir Alex Ferguson
Record attendance:	70,504 v Aston Villa, 27 Dec 1920, Div One
Record League victory:	10-1 v Wolves, 15 Oct 1892, Div One
Record Cup victory:	10-0 v RSC Anderlecht, 26 Sept 1956, European Cup Preliminary Round second leg
Record defeat:	0-7 v Blackburn R, 10 April 1926, Div One; 0-7 v Aston Villa, 27 Dec 1930, Div One; 0-7 v Wolves, 26 Dec 1931, Div Two
Most League goals (season):	Dennis Viollet, 32, 1959-60, Div One
Most League goals (career):	Bobby Charlton, 199, 1956-73
Most League appearances:	Bobby Charlton, 606, 1956-73

team featuring Charlton, Kidd and Best. Now Scholes, Schmeichel, Stam and company had their own place in United – and soccer's – Hall of Fame.

The Premiership was reclaimed from Arsenal after a titanic battle, gracing the Old Trafford trophy cabinet for the fifth time in the competition's seven-year history. The FA Cup followed hard on its heels, victory against Newcastle coming as an anti-climax after a clash with holders Arsenal that went to two games and extra time before it was decided by a Ryan Giggs wondergoal. And the big one, the European Cup (or Champions League, as it's nowadays called) was claimed in the palatial surroundings of Barcelona's Nou Camp stadium. Moreover, it was snatched from the grasp of Bayern Munich, a team hailing from the city where the United airliner crashed in 1958, wiping out a generation of players.

The club began life in 1878 as Newton Heath, formed by workers from the Lancashire and Yorkshire Railways. They were promoted to the First Division, then the top flight, but the early years were a struggle, and their first ground at North Road, Newton Heath, was no Old Trafford. It had no changing facilities and a mudbath for a pitch: many visiting clubs complained about its state.

Relegated to the Second Division, they battled to stay alive and, under new ownership, changed their name to Manchester United in 1902. New funds were found for transfers and the first of United's great players, Billy Meredith, was signed from Manchester City.

Historians have dubbed Meredith, nicknamed the Welsh Wizard, the George Best or David Beckham of the Edwardian era. He certainly ushered in a successful period, helping win promotion to the First Division. The League Championship came in 1908 and

1911, their first FA Cup in 1909, and success allowed the club to make the move to a purpose-built stadium at Old Trafford. Holding 60,000 people, it was a ground fit for Champions.

When the League resumed after World War One, enthusiasm was at a peak and in 1920, 70,504 people – a club record to this day – crammed into Old Trafford to see United play Aston Villa. But United were relegated to the Second Division in 1922 – and, although they bounced back in 1925, they entered a very lean period. Only 11,000 people watched Newcastle thrash United at Old Trafford in a 1930-31 season where they lost 27 games and won only seven. The rest of the 1930s were spent in relegation and promotion between the divisions.

War again suspended League football until 1946, and when peace resumed Old Trafford was a bombsite. It would be three years before United would play at home again – but in former Company Sergeant Major Instructor Matt Busby the club had found the man to lead them to glory.

The team Busby created showed the promise that had been lacking in the 1920s and 1930s. The strike force of Jack Rowley and Stan Pearson shot them to FA Cup victory for the second time ever, the club's first major honour for 37 years.

The 1950s were a golden era for United, Matt Busby and his 'Babes', three Championships being won in a decade tinged with tragedy as well as triumph. The Munich air crash of 6 February 1958 cruelly cut short the lives of eight young United players and 13 other officials and pressmen travelling back from Belgrade after a European Cup Quarter-Final. The country mourned the loss of such young talents as Tommy Taylor, Duncan Edwards and Roger Byrne, while Busby himself hovered between life and death.

Peter Schmeichel ▶

HONOURS BOARD

1896-97 Div Two Runners-up	1975-76 FA Cup Runners-up
1905-06 Div Two Runners-up	1976-77 FA Cup Winners
1907-08 Div One Champions	1978-79 FA Cup Runners-up
1908-09 FA Cup Winners	1979-80 Div One Runners-up
1910-11 Div One Champions	1982-83 FA Cup Winners and
1924-25 Div Two Runners-up	League Cup Runners-up
1935-36 Div Two Champions	1984-85 FA Cup Winners
1937-38 Div Two Runners-up	1987-88 Div One Runners-up
1946-47 Div One Runners-up	1989-90 FA Cup Winners
1947-48 Div One Runners-up	1990-91 League Cup Runners-up,
and FA Cup Winners	European Cup Winners'
1948-49 Div One Runners-up	Cup Winners and Super
1950-51 Div One Runners-up	Cup Winners
1951-52 Div One Champions	1991-92 Div One Runners-up and
1955-56 Div One Champions	League Cup Winners
1956-57 Div One Champions and	1992-93 Premiership Champions
FA Cup Runners-up	1993-94 Premiership Champions,
1957-58 FA Cup Runners-up	FA Cup Winners and
1958-59 Div One Runners-up	League Cup Runners-up
1962-63 FA Cup Winners	1994-95 Premiership Runners-up
1963-64 Div One Runners-up	and FA Cup Runners-up
1964-65 Div One Champions	1995-96 Premiership Champions
1966-67 Div One Champions	and FA Cup Winners
1967-68 Div One Runners-up,	1996-97 Premiership Champions
European Cup Winners,	1997-98 Premiership Runners-up
World Club Championship	1998-99 Premiership Champions,
Runners-up	FA Cup Winners and
1974-75 Div Two Champions	European Cup Winners

United put out a scratch team in the FA Cup Final and lost to Bolton, but Busby knew he had to rebuild. His signings in the early 1960s included Denis Law (for a British record £115,000) and a young man from Northern Ireland called George Best whose talent would be at the centre of United's 1960s glory years.

Bobby Charlton's inspired leadership on the pitch was one of the factors that brought United FA Cup victory in 1963 and Championships in 1965 and 1967. But it was the historic 1968 European Cup victory against Benfica at Wembley that was United's and Busby's crowning achievement. Ten years after Munich, the ambition was achieved and Busby retired in 1969 after 23 years in charge.

The club went through a procession of managers through the early 1970s as Best left and Charlton retired. The lowest point came in 1974 when United were relegated for the first time in 37 years. Tommy Docherty brought them back to the top flight but the team lost to Second Division Southampton in the 1976 FA Cup Final. United returned to Wembley the following year and won the Cup, beating the then all-conquering Liverpool.

The next decade saw Dave Sexton and Ron Atkinson try and fail to make a lasting mark, though Atkinson brought Captain Marvel, Bryan Robson, to Old Trafford. Robson was expensive at a record £1.5 million, but proved to be one of the greatest ever United players.

Two Cup Finals were reached in 1983, and though the Red Devils lost to Liverpool in the League Cup Final they came back two months later to play Brighton, winning 4-0 in a replay. The FA Cup followed in 1985 with a 1-0 win against Everton, but for all their character and talent Ron Atkinson's side had not won a Championship.

Gritty Scot Alex Ferguson, previously manager of Aberdeen, entered the Theatre of Dreams in 1986. His first three seasons brought little, but since the Red Devils took off again with an FA Cup win in 1990 they have dominated the English domestic game in the way Liverpool dominated the late 1970s and 1980s. Players like Hughes, Ince, Pallister and Giggs became household names with their international-class performances.

As the decade continued, a team built around mercurial Frenchman Eric Cantona and increasingly featuring home-grown youngsters like David Beckham, Paul Scholes, Nicky Butt and the Neville brothers, Gary and Phil, has personified the renaissance of English football. United recorded two League and Cup Doubles, the only English club ever to achieve the feat, and took four of the first five Premierships, but critics claimed the retirement of Cantona would bring an end to the glory days. How wrong could they be? Fergie's Fledglings have proved themselves the equals of the Busby Babes, and their historic Treble may never be equalled.

The future looks bright, too, with young defensive prodigy Wes Brown already an England international, Dutchman Jaap Stam the rock of the defence and £12 million Tobagan Dwight York forming a superb spearhead with Andy Cole. Between the posts, eight-season veteran Peter Schmeichel, the best goalkeeper United have ever fielded, has already been replaced by Australian Mark Bosnich. There's little doubt that, with the World Team Championship now added to United's targets, that all members of the squad will play a vital role as United enter the next millennium as Britain – if not Europe, or the world's – leading club side. Fergie's Red Army just goes marching on and on…

Jaap Stam ▶

1999-2000 FIXTURES

FA Carling Premiership

Date	Opponents	Venue	Previous Results 98-99	97-98	96-97
Aug 8	Everton	(A)	4-1	2-0	2-0
11	Sheffield Wednesday	(H)	3-0	6-1	2-0
14	Leeds Utd	(H)	3-2	3-0	1-0
22	Arsenal	(A)	0-3	2-3	2-1
25	Coventry City	(A)	1-0	2-3	2-0
28	Newcastle United	(H)	0-0	1-1	0-0
Sept 11	Liverpool	(A)	2-2	3-1	3-1
18	Wimbledon	(H)	5-1	2-0	2-1
25	Southampton	(H)	2-1	1-0	2-1
Oct 3	Chelsea	(A)	0-0	1-0	1-1
16	Watford	(H)	—	—	—
23	Tottenham Hotspur	(A)	2-2	2-0	2-1
30	Aston Villa	(A)	2-1	1-0	0-0
Nov 6	Leicester City	(H)	2-2	0-1	3-1
20	Derby County	(A)	1-1	2-2	1-1
27	Sheffield Wednesday	(A)	1-3	0-2	1-1
Dec 4	Everton	(H)	3-1	2-0	2-2
18	West Ham United	(H)	0-0	1-1	2-2
26	Bradford City	(H)	—	—	—
28	Sunderland	(A)	—	—	1-2
Jan 3	Middlesbrough	(H)	2-3	—	3-3
15	Leeds United	(A)	1-1	0-1	4-0
22	Arsenal	(H)	1-1	0-1	1-0
Feb 5	Coventry City	(H)	2-0	3-0	3-1
12	Newcastle United	(A)	2-1	1-0	0-5
26	Wimbledon	(A)	1-1	5-2	3-0
Mar 4	Liverpool	(H)	2-0	1-1	1-0

1999-2000 FIXTURES

11	Derby County	(H)	1-0	2-0	2-3
18	Leicester City	(A)	6-2	0-0	2-2
25	Bradford City	(A)	—	—	—
Apr 1	West Ham United	(H)	4-1	2-1	2-0
8	Middlesbrough	(A)	1-0	—	2-2
15	Sunderland	(H)	—	—	5-0
22	Southampton	(A)	3-0	0-1	3-6
24	Chelsea	(H)	1-1	2-2	1-2
29	Watford	(A)	—	—	—
May 6	Tottenham Hotspur	(H)	2-1	2-0	2-0
14	Aston Villa	(A)	1-1	2-0	0-0

Axa FA Cup

Dec 11	Third Round
Jan 8	Fourth Round
29	Fifth Round
Feb 19	Sixth Round
Apr 9	Semi-Final
May 20	Final

Worthington Cup

Oct 13	Third Round
Dec 1	Fourth Round
15	Fifth Round
Jan 12	Semi-Final 1
26	Semi-Final 2
Feb 27	Final

UEFA Champions League

Sep 15	Phase One 1
22	Phase One 2
29	Phase One 3
Oct 20	Phase One 4
27	Phase One 5
Nov 3	Phase One 6
24	Phase Two 1
Dec 8	Phase Two 2
Mar 1	Phase Two 3
8	Phase Two 4
15	Phase Two 5
22	Phase Two 6
Apr 5	Quarter-Final 1
19	Quarter-Final 2
May 3	Semi-Final 1
10	Semi-Final 2
24	Final

26 Monday

27 Tuesday

28 Wednesday

29 Thursday

30 Friday

31 Saturday

1 Sunday

FA Charity Shield: Arsenal v Man United

Season Week 1

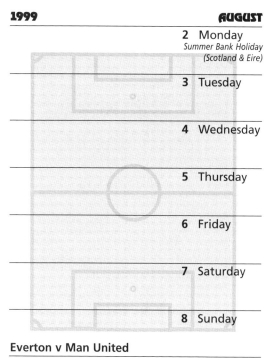

2   Monday
Summer Bank Holiday
(Scotland & Eire)

3   Tuesday

4   Wednesday

5   Thursday

6   Friday

7   Saturday

8   Sunday

Everton v Man United

Season Week 2

AUGUST ACTION

This Time Last Year...

After the unpleasant shock of a Charity Shield reverse to Arsenal, it was back to Old Trafford and a capacity crowd for the serious business of reclaiming the Premiership title. But everything went pear-shaped, and it took a last-minute Beckham blast to deprive lowly Leicester of all three points! A no-score draw at Upton Park was more like it, but the biggest news of August 1998 was safe passage through the Qualifying Round of the Champions League thanks to goals from Giggs and Cole – the first steps on a legendary journey!

Thrills To Come...

This season brings a repeat of the Arsenal clash at Wembley – revenge would be sweet, now the trophies are back at Old Trafford! – plus no fewer than six Premiership fixtures, including back-to-back testers against Leeds and Arsenal. Then it's all off to Monte Carlo for a European Super Cup date with Lazio...Salas, Anelka and all!

This Month Last Season

Date	Comp	Venue	Opposition	Result
9	CS	N	Arsenal	0-3
12	EC	H	LKS Lodz	2-0
15	PL	H	Leicester C	2-2
22	PL	A	West Ham Utd	0-0
26	EC	A	LKS Lodz	0-0

David Beckham/Dwight Yorke

9 Monday

10 Tuesday

*Roy Keane born in
Cork, Eire (1971).*

11 Wednesday

Man United v Sheffield Wed

12 Thursday

13 Friday

14 Saturday

Man United v Leeds United

15 Sunday

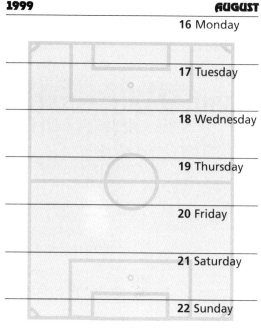

16 Monday

17 Tuesday

18 Wednesday

19 Thursday

20 Friday

21 Saturday

22 Sunday

Arsenal v Man United

23 Monday

24 Tuesday

25 Wednesday

Coventry C v Man United

26 Thursday

27 Friday

**European Super Cup:
Lazio v Man United**

28 Saturday

Man United v Newcastle United

29 Sunday

30 Monday
Summer Bank Holiday
(England, Wales & NI)

31 Tuesday

Henning Berg born in
Eidsvoll, Norway (1968).

1 Wednesday

2 Thursday

John Curtis born in Nuneaton
(1978). Ryan Ford born in
Worksop (1978).

3 Friday

4 Saturday

5 Sunday

SEPTEMBER ACTION

This Time Last Year...

September '98 saw United get into their stride. Charlton were shown how tough the Premiership is, with Dwight Yorke scoring his first goals in a 4-1 win, while it's always nice to put one over on Liverpool! The Arsenal bogey continued, but three Premiership wins out of four was the kind of form Fergie wanted to see. Back in Europe, Barcelona visited the Theatre of Dreams and all but caused an upset! United, 2-0 up at half-time, were grateful to share six goals in a thriller. A 2-2 draw in Munich was much more creditable, Yorke scoring his first European goal in a red shirt. His partnership with Andy Cole was already looking Championship class...

Thrills To Come...

This season United have Liverpool, Wimbledon and Southampton in their domestic sights, while their defence of the Champions Cup kicks off with three Phase One games.

This Month Last Season

Date	Comp	Venue	Opposition	Result
9	PL	H	Charlton Ath	4-1
12	PL	H	Coventry C	2-0
16	EC	H	Barcelona	3-3
20	PL	A	Arsenal	0-3
24	PL	H	Liverpool	2-0
30	EC	A	Bayern Munich	2-2

Ole Gunnar Solskjaer

6 Monday

---

7 Tuesday

---

8 Wednesday

---

9 Thursday

---

10 Friday   *Ronnie Wallwork born in Manchester (1977).*

---

11 Saturday   *United's first European match, v Anderlecht (1956).*

Liverpool v Man United

---

12 Sunday

---

13 Monday

George Best makes his United debut v West Brom (1963).

14 Tuesday

15 Wednesday

Champions League Phase One 1

16 Thursday

17 Friday

18 Saturday

Man United v Wimbledon

19 Sunday

20 Monday

21 Tuesday   *Jamie Wood born in*
                                Salford (1978).

22 Wednesday

Champions League Phase One 2

23 Thursday

24 Friday

25 Saturday

Man United v Southampton

26 Sunday   *Record Cup victory: 10-0*
                                v Anderlecht (1956).

27 Monday

28 Tuesday

29 Wednesday

Champions League Phase One 3

30 Thursday

Duncan Edwards born in Dudley (1936).   **1** Friday

2 Saturday

First Manchester derby in the FA Cup (1891).   **3** Sunday

Chelsea v Man United

OCTOBER ACTION

This Time Last Year...

An unbeaten month last season in all competitions will be hard to beat this time round, though we're going to enjoy seeing United try! The highlights were three demolition jobs: Wimbledon and Everton in the League, and Brondby – Peter Schmeichel's former team – in the European Cup. Seven United players made the scoresheet in those three games alone, suggesting goals to come from all parts of the field. As Alex Ferguson rotated his squad, Jordi Cruyff made the most of a rare sub appearance to score a late equaliser against Derby at Pride Park, the only dropped points in an excellent month.

Thrills To Come...

This October brings its own challenges, including capital trips to Stamford Bridge and White Hart Lane plus a visit from Watford, their first since 1988.

This Month Last Season

Date	Comp	Venue	Opposition	Result
3	PL	A	Southampton	3-0
17	PL	H	Wimbledon	5-1
21	EC	A	Brondby	6-2
24	PL	A	Derby Co	1-1
28	WC	H	Bury	2-0
31	PL	A	Everton	4-1

Jesper Blomqvist ▶

OCTOBER **1999**

4 Monday

5 Tuesday

6 Wednesday

7 Thursday

8 Friday

9 Saturday

10 Sunday

Season Week 11

Sir Bobby Charlton born in Ashington (1937).

11 Monday

12 Tuesday

Wes Brown born in Manchester (1979).

Worthington Cup Third Round

13 Wednesday

14 Thursday

Andy Cole born in Nottingham (1971).

15 Friday

16 Saturday

Man United v Watford

17 Sunday

18 Monday

19 Tuesday

20 Wednesday

Champions League Phase One 4

21 Thursday

22 Friday

23 Saturday

Tottenham H v Man United

24 Sunday
Summer Time Ends

25 Monday
October Day (Eire only)

26 Tuesday

27 Wednesday

Champions League Phase One 5

28 Thursday

29 Friday

30 Saturday

Man United v Aston Villa

*Denis Irwin born in
Cork, Eire (1965).*

31 Sunday
Hallowe'en

This Time Last Year...

Having scraped past neighbours Bury, the reserves – sorry Worthington Cup side – beat Nottingham Forest to progress to Round Three. European glory stayed on the agenda, a second thrashing of Brondby followed, amazingly, by another 3-3 see-saw draw against Barcelona, this time at the Nou Camp. The Premiership month was average by comparison – two wins, one draw and a defeat at Hillsborough, only the second of the campaign.

Thrills To Come...

Apart from European matters this month, United will be visiting Sheffield Wednesday again (and hoping for revenge!), plus Midlands clashes with Leicester and Derby. Last but not least comes the Toyota World Cup in Tokyo against Brazilians Palmeiras.

This Month Last Season

Date	Comp	Venue	Opposition	Result
4	EC	H	Brondby	5-0
8	PL	H	Newcastle Utd	0-0
11	WC	H	Nott'm Forest	2-1
14	PL	H	Blackburn R	3-2
21	PL	A	Sheffield Wed	1-3
25	EC	A	Barcelona	3-3
29	PL	H	Leeds Utd	3-2

David Beckham ▶

1 Monday

2 Tuesday

3 Wednesday   *Dwight Yorke born in*
Tobago (1971).

Champions League Phase One 6

4 Thursday

5 Friday
Guy Fawkes Night

6 Saturday   *Alex Ferguson arrives at Old*
Trafford as manager (1986).

Man United v Leicester C

7 Sunday
Remembrance Sunday

8 Monday

9 Tuesday

Erik Nevland born in   **10** Wednesday
Stavanger, Norway (1977).

11 Thursday

12 Friday

13 Saturday

14 Sunday

15 Monday

16 Tuesday   *Paul Scholes born in*
Salford (1974).

17 Wednesday

18 Thursday   *Peter Schmeichel born in*
Gladsaxe, Denmark (1963).

19 Friday

20 Saturday

                                  Derby Co v Man United

21 Sunday

22 Monday

23 Tuesday

24 Wednesday

Champions League Phase Two 1

25 Thursday

*Eric Cantona signed
from Leeds (1992).*

26 Friday

27 Saturday

Sheffield Wed v Man United

28 Sunday

DECEMBER ACTION

This Time Last Year…

Another even-honours month in the Premiership – four draws, a win and a defeat – made December 1998 less than memorable. Add defeat in the Worthington Cup, though to the eventual winners, and a draw at home against Bayern Munich (this after Roy Keane had got United's nose in front) and you have what, by United's high standards, was a disappointing way to end the year. The defeat at home to Boro would, however, prove their last of the campaign.

Thrills To Come…

Two of the three promoted clubs – Bradford City and Sunderland – have the opportunity to measure their progress this month. This will be United's first visit to the Stadium of Light, an Old Trafford in miniature.

This Month Last Season				
Date	**Comp**	**Venue**	**Opposition**	**Result**
2	WC	A	Tottenham H	1-3
5	PL	A	Aston Villa	1-1
9	EC	H	Bayern Munich	1-1
12	PL	A	Tottenham H	2-2
16	PL	H	Chelsea	1-1
19	PL	H	Middlesbrough	2-3
26	PL	H	Nott'm Forest	3-0
29	PL	A	Chelsea	0-0

Roy Keane ▶

29 Monday

*Ryan Giggs born in
Cardiff (1973).*

30 Tuesday
St Andrew's Day

Toyota World Cup
Man United v Palmeiras

1 Wednesday

Worthington Cup Fourth Round

2 Thursday

3 Friday

4 Saturday

Man United v Everton

5 Sunday

Season Week 19

6 Monday

7 Tuesday

8 Wednesday

Champions League Phase Two 2

9 Thursday

Alex Notman born in Edinburgh (1979).

10 Friday

11 Saturday

FA Cup Third Round

12 Sunday

13 Monday

14 Tuesday

15 Wednesday

Worthington Cup Fifth Round

16 Thursday

17 Friday

18 Saturday

West Ham United v Man United

19 Sunday

20 Monday

21 Tuesday
Winter Solstice

22 Wednesday

23 Thursday

24 Friday

25 Saturday
Christmas Day

Michael Twiss born in Salford (1977).

Man United v Bradford C

26 Sunday
Boxing Day (UK & NI)
St Stephen's Day (Eire)

JANUARY ACTION

This Time Last Year...

The month the FA Cup trail started in earnest. Middlesbrough discovered their December win was a one-off, leaving Old Trafford soundly beaten, while Liverpool made their second visit of the season and, though they thought they'd won it, crashed to Yorke and Solskjaer strikes in the 88th and 90th minutes. Explosive ends to matches couldn't come more dramatic than that…could they? Premiership-wise, three wins out of three with a total of 11 goals scored made January as good a month as December had been disappointing.

Thrills To Come...

The idea of facing Leeds and Arsenal would make the first month of the new Millennium a memorable one. But United, of course, have more on their minds this time round. With the World Team Championships kicking off on 5 January they'll be in even more of a global spotlight than usual.

This Month Last Season

Date	Comp	Venue	Opposition	Result
3	FAC	H	Middlesbrough	3-1
10	PL	H	West Ham Utd	4-1
16	PL	A	Leicester C	6-2
24	FAC	H	Liverpool	2-1
31	PL	A	Charlton Ath	1-0

Jaap Stam ▶

27 Monday
Bank Holiday

Record attendance of 70,504 v Aston Villa (1920). Joint record defeat: 7-0 v Aston Villa (1930).

28 Tuesday
Bank Holiday

Paul Teather born in Rotherham (1977).

Sunderland v Man United

29 Wednesday

Danny Higginbotham born in Manchester (1978).

30 Thursday

31 Friday
Bank Holiday

Sir Alex Ferguson born in Glasgow (1941).

1 Saturday
New Year's Day

2 Sunday

Jonathan Greening born in Scarborough (1979).

3   Monday
Bank Holiday

Man United v Middlesbrough

4   Tuesday
Bank Holiday (Scotland only)

5   Wednesday

World Team Championships

6   Thursday

7   Friday

8   Saturday

FA Cup Fourth Round

9   Sunday

10 Monday

11 Tuesday

12 Wednesday

Worthington Cup Semi-Final 1

13 Thursday

*Mark Bosnich born in
Fairfield, Australia (1972).*

14 Friday

15 Saturday

Leeds United v Man United

16 Sunday

17 Monday

18 Tuesday

19 Wednesday

Legendary manager Sir Matt Busby dies (1994).

20 Thursday

Nicky Butt born in Manchester (1975). Phil Neville born in Bury (1977).

21 Friday

22 Saturday

Man United v Arsenal

23 Sunday

FEBRUARY ACTION

This Time Last Year...

The month of February belonged to one man – Ole Gunnar Solskjaer, whose four goals in 11 minutes (80, 87, 90, 90) put relegation-bound Nottingham Forest to the sword. Derby, Coventry and Southampton were the other scalps, Dwight Yorke picking up four goals in the month, while a draw with Arsenal at least improved on the two previous meetings! The FA Cup brought Kevin Keegan's Fulham to Old Trafford, where a Cole goal proved sufficient to ensure Fergie's Red Army went marching on towards Wembley.

Thrills To Come...

The Worthington Cup Final could be an important date this year, if adding to the three trophies already under lock and key at Old Trafford is important. Otherwise, look forward to testing trips to St James' and Selhurst Parks while Coventry are the sole League visitors to Old Trafford.

This Month Last Season

Date	Comp	Venue	Opposition	Result
3	PL	H	Derby Co	1-0
6	PL	A	Nott'm Forest	8-1
14	FAC	H	Fulham	1-0
17	PL	H	Arsenal	1-1
20	PL	A	Coventry C	1-0
27	PL	H	Southampton	2-1

Andy Cole ▶

24 Monday

25 Tuesday

26 Wednesday

Worthington Cup Semi-Final 2

27 Thursday

28 Friday

29 Saturday

FA Cup Fifth Round

30 Sunday

31 Monday

1 Tuesday

2 Wednesday

3 Thursday

4 Friday

Jesper Blomqvist born in Tavelsjo, Sweden (1974).

Man United v Coventry C

5 Saturday

Munich air disaster (1958).

6 Sunday

7 Monday

8 Tuesday

9 Wednesday *Jordi Cruyff born in Amsterdam, Holland (1974). Mark Wilson born in Scunthorpe (1979).*

10 Thursday

11 Friday

12 Saturday

Newcastle United v Man United

13 Sunday

14 Monday

*Matt Busby appointed
manager (1945).*   **15** Tuesday

16 Wednesday

17 Thursday

*Gary Neville born in
Bury (1975).*   **18** Friday

*First match played at
Old Trafford (1910).*   **19** Saturday

FA Cup Sixth Round

20 Sunday

21 Monday

22 Tuesday

23 Wednesday
Ash Wednesday

24 Thursday

Denis Law born in Aberdeen (1940).

25 Friday

26 Saturday

Ole Gunnar Solskjaer born in Kristiansund, Norway (1973).

Wimbledon v Man United

27 Sunday

Worthington Cup Final

28 Monday

29 Tuesday

1 Wednesday
St David's Day

Champions League Phase Two 3

2 Thursday

3 Friday

United hammer　　　　**4** Saturday
Ipswich 9-0 (1995).

Man United v Liverpool

5 Sunday

6 Monday

7 Tuesday

8 Wednesday

Champions League Phase Two 4

9 Thursday

10 Friday

11 Saturday

Man United v Derby Co

12 Sunday

13 Monday

14 Tuesday

15 Wednesday

Champions League Phase Two 5

16 Thursday

17 Friday
St Patrick's Day (NI & Eire)

18 Saturday

Leicester C v Man United

19 Sunday
Mothering Sunday

20 Monday

21 Tuesday

22 Wednesday

Champions League Phase Two 6

23 Thursday

24 Friday   *Rai Van Der Gouw born in Oldenzaal, Holland (1963).*

25 Saturday

Bradford C v Man United

26 Sunday
Summer Time Begins

Season Week 35

27 Monday

28 Tuesday

29 Wednesday

30 Thursday

31 Friday

1 Saturday
All Fools' Day

Man United v West Ham United

Teddy Sheringham born in London (1966).

2 Sunday

This Time Last Year...

Juventus proved worthy Semi-Final opponents, and nearly emerged from Old Trafford with a win. Ryan Giggs' 90th-minute goal pulled things level, and an epic 3-2 victory in Turin (United's first on Italian soil) put a Final place beyond argument. Premiership form stuttered with two draws and a win, but it was Arsenal who provided the sternest test as United's bid for the Treble seemed set to founder in the FA Cup Semi-Final. All looked lost when the Gunners pulled back a 1-0 lead in the Semi-Final replay, but Ryan Giggs' 109th-minute goal sparked celebrations a-plenty!

Thrills To Come...

It's Champions League Quarter-Final month, surrounded by tricky away games at Middlesbrough, Southampton and Watford.

This Month Last Season

Date	Comp	Venue	Opposition	Result
3	PL	A	Wimbledon	1-1
7	EC	H	Juventus	1-1
10	FAC	N	Arsenal	0-0
14	FAC	N	Arsenal	2-1
17	PL	H	Sheffield Wed	3-0
21	EC	A	Juventus	3-2
25	PL	A	Leeds Utd	1-1

Ryan Giggs ▶

3 Monday

4 Tuesday

5 Wednesday

Champions League Quarter-Final 1

6 Thursday

7 Friday

8 Saturday

Middlesbrough v Man United

9 Sunday

FA Cup Semi-Final

Joint record defeat: 7-0 v
Blackburn R (1926).

10 Monday

11 Tuesday

12 Wednesday

13 Thursday

14 Friday

15 Saturday

Man United v Sunderland

16 Sunday
Palm Sunday

17 Monday

18 Tuesday

19 Wednesday

Champions League Quarter-Final 2

20 Thursday

21 Friday
Good Friday Bank Holiday

22 Saturday

Southampton v Man United

23 Sunday
St George's Day

24 Monday

Easter Monday Bank Holiday

Man United v Chelsea

25 Tuesday

26 Wednesday

United play QPR in the first ever **27** Thursday
Charity Shield match (1908).

A Denis Law goal relegates **28** Friday
United to the Second Division
(1974).

29 Saturday

Watford v Man United

30 Sunday

1 Monday
May Day Holiday

2 Tuesday

*David Beckham born
in London (1975).*

3 Wednesday

Champions League Semi-Final 1

4 Thursday

5 Friday

6 Saturday

Man United v Tottenham H

7 Sunday

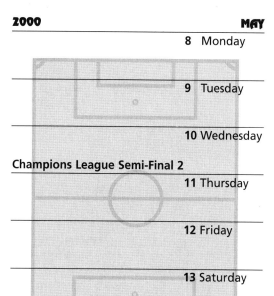

8 Monday

9 Tuesday

10 Wednesday

Champions League Semi-Final 2

11 Thursday

12 Friday

13 Saturday

14 Sunday

Aston Villa v Man United

MAY ACTION

This Time Last Year...

May 1999 was, of course, the most glorious month in United's long and proud history. In the space of just two weeks, the historic Treble of Premiership, FA Cup and European Cup was secured, ensuring the team equal status with Best, Law, Charlton and co and earning Alex Ferguson a well deserved knighthood. Newcastle were put in their place at Wembley despite Roy Keane's early injury, while sub Teddy Sheringham notched United's first in both Finals to cement his own personal place in history.

Thrills To Come...

What could top the events of just 12 months ago? We'll just have to wait and see, but with two European Semi-Finals and a Final there'll be more than enough chance for all squad members, like Teddy, to write their name in the record books.

This Month Last Season

Date	Comp	Venue	Opposition	Result
1	PL	H	Aston Villa	2-1
5	PL	A	Liverpool	2-2
9	PL	A	Middlesbrough	1-0
12	PL	A	Blackburn R	1-1
16	PL	H	Tottenham H	2-1
22	FAC	N	Newcastle Utd	2-0
26	EC	N	Bayern Munich	2-1

Ole Gunnar Solskjaer ▶

15 Monday   *United win the Cup Winners'*
                                 Cup against Barcelona (1991).

16 Tuesday   *United are crowned Premiership*
                        Champions for the fifth time in
                                 seven years (1999).

17 Wednesday

18 Thursday

19 Friday

20 Saturday

                                              FA Cup Final

21 Sunday

George Best born in Belfast (1946). United beat Newcastle 2-0 to win the Double (1999).

22 Monday

23 Tuesday

Eric Cantona born in Paris, France (1966).

Champions League Final

24 Wednesday

25 Thursday

Sir Matt Busby born near Glasgow (1909). United beat Bayern Munich 2-1 to clinch the Treble (1999).

26 Friday

27 Saturday

28 Sunday

29 Monday   *European Cup Final triumph*
Spring Bank Holiday (UK & NI)   *over Benfica (1968).*

30 Tuesday

31 Wednesday

1 Thursday

2 Friday

3 Saturday

4 Sunday

Close Season Week 1

5 Monday
June Holiday (Eire only)

6 Tuesday

7 Wednesday

8 Thursday

9 Friday

Ronny Johnsen born in Sandefjord, Norway (1969).

10 Saturday

11 Sunday

QUESTION TIME

1. Who scored the goal that brought the European Cup back to Old Trafford for the first time in 31 years?
2. Apart from United, which club has Alex Ferguson led to triumph in Europe?
3. Where was keeper Mark Bosnich born?
4. United claimed three Doubles in the 1990s. Name the sides they beat in the FA Cup Finals...
5. Who holds United's League appearance record?
6. When did United take up residence at Old Trafford?
7. From which team did Alex Ferguson sign Jaap Stam?
8. Old Trafford waved farewell to legendary goalkeeper Peter Schmeichel during the 1999 close season: which club did he join on a free transfer?
9. What is United's own television channel called?
10. Which United star scored a hat-trick at Wembley in March 1999?
11. Which trophy did the Football Association allow United not to defend this season?
12. Which former United favourite found his new team relegated from the Premiership in May?
13. The whole of Manchester were celebrating in May 1999. Why?
14. Which former United favourite found himself in charge of his national side last summer?
15. Which England international scored one goal and made another in the 1999 FA Cup Final?

(More questions opposite)

(Continued)

16. Who is United's assistant manager?
17. Which team will United face in the European Super Cup?
18. Which was the last team to beat United during 1998-99?
19. Victory over which team gave United their first European Cup triumph?
20. Nottingham Forest were hit for how many goals over the course of three matches last season?
21. Which player topped the Old Trafford scoring charts last season?
22. Who tried to buy Manchester United last season?
23. Where will United compete in the World Team Championship in January 2000?
24. How many times have United won the FA Cup?
25. Name the only club to beat United twice last season...
26. Who scored United's first goal of the 1998-99 campaign?
27. Which former United winger helped Bradford to reach the top flight for the first time in 77 years?
28. How did David Beckham make headlines in July 1999?
29. Which two United midfielders were forced to sit out the European Cup Final through suspension?
30. How many different players did Alex Ferguson field in all competitions during 1998-99?

(Answers on last page)

12 Monday

Alex Ferguson is knighted in the Queen's Birthday Honours (1998).

13 Tuesday

14 Wednesday

15 Thursday

16 Friday

17 Saturday

18 Sunday
Father's Day

Close Season Week 3

19 Monday

Peter Schmeichel signs for Sporting Lisbon (1999).

20 Tuesday

21 Wednesday
Summer Solstice

22 Thursday

23 Friday

David May born in Oldham (1970).

24 Saturday

25 Sunday

26 Monday

27 Tuesday

28 Wednesday

29 Thursday

30 Friday

1 Saturday

2 Sunday

Close Season Week 5

Michael Clegg born in Tameside (1977).   **3**   Monday

4   Tuesday

5   Wednesday

Nick Culkin born in York (1978).   **6**   Thursday

7   Friday

8   Saturday

9   Sunday

10 Monday

11 Tuesday

12 Wednesday
Battle of the Boyne (NI)

13 Thursday

14 Friday

15 Saturday

16 Sunday

Close Season Week 7

Jaap Stam born in Kampen, Holland (1972).

17 Monday

18 Tuesday

19 Wednesday

20 Thursday

21 Friday

22 Saturday

23 Sunday

24 Monday

25 Tuesday

26 Wednesday

27 Thursday

28 Friday

29 Saturday

30 Sunday

United stars Charlton and Stiles help England win the World Cup at Wembley (1966).